THE REPERCEPTION OF CIRCADIAN RHYTHM

Sleep, eat, drink, love, reproduce, travel and poetry revisited

By

Steven G. Deaton

ISBN: 1-4033-5311-5 (e-book)
ISBN: 1-4033-5312-3 (Paperback)

This book is printed on acid free paper.

1stBooks - rev. 09/21/02

For

D. Elizabeth LaClair

Our watches were in sync once, maybe twice, Okay, three times

Contents

Sunday Night is the Worst

Eleven thirty-five

Between noon and midnight

Through the glass

The Portland rain.

Me and the city of roses

Are lying down

Anxiety sleeps over

Only on Sunday,

Invading the present wish

To be still

With

Spears, smoke, arrows, cannon balls

And pistol-whips

Across the bow of Monday

Making every sound

City symphony Monday thru Saturday

Now eerie exaggerated

Exasperated

On the street below my bedroom window

Someone honks only once.

A simple chorus

A sharp

Distinctly familiar call to mate

Piercing the hoary night

The audience quiet

Waiting for the one

Cymbal

Apartment door to slam

And the orchestrated notes

Like a doe

Running for the iron buck

Idling in youthful shelter below

Dodging hunters arrows

Brushing branches thrashing hallways

Determined with pancake anxiety

And lipstick commitment

To the anticipation

Of a different meaning

To an ordinary flight

Across the fearful distance

From here to there.

I know this opera.

I played in it when I was young

On the street below

Someone's bedroom window

Calling out in the night

My urgency, my recklessness

My hungry passion

Untamed and playing tricks on my mind.

Rain and Sunday be damned.

Like Kerosene on flame

It exaggerates the danger

It exasperates the intent.

One horn

Nothing else matters

Till it's done

And she's back where I found her

I can sleep.

Now, in the shelter of age

Once disturbed

And unsure

I just roll over

Put my arm around her

And

Pull her close.

Steven G. Deaton

He Built His Own House, He loved us to call it Home

My father

Can't keep his food down

Anymore.

That phone call

Rings

Chills

Down

The spiritual kind

From both sides of the fence.

I will not carry on

His good name

My brothers and sisters

Will

Forgive me. I was always happy

To see him

From a divided distance

There was my

Divorces, my selfish directions, my flights.

His calm, his power

His undivided attention

Even with his marriage, his children

His selfless directions

How could I have come from him

To become me?

I cannot give back

All that I have taken

I want to scream

But

I can only find peace with him

In a quieter way.

Steven G. Deaton

Hell Yes or No

I close my eyes

And everything

I mean everything

Parades around

The streets of the stadium

Of one game or another

Like floats

Of flowers stuffed in chicken wire

And young girls

Dressed like public desire

Waving to me

With promises of today and tomorrow.

Smiles

With hollowed passion

Untruths

They don't know

Up and down the streets

Of one weekend or another

City this and city that

Yearning

For acceptance or

Another chance

All I ever had to do

Was

Flip a coin

Tails its hell no

Heads its hell yes.

Vegas Virga

Everyone watches looks and listens

For the call to pardon

They pace the floor

And the streets

Paroled from routine and sacrifice

No limits to apologize for

And

No escape from the pittance and the pother.

Dorothy was outside

The current of the Casino electric chairs

Which fried me the

Night before.

Waiting in her bare feet

Her shoes produced a blister

The size of Nevada

She couldn't walk the strip.

Perfect desert night

Cool wind whispering winner

In my ear

I left her on the corner

Of jackpot and despair.

I carried Cinderella's slippers

Across the desert floor

Past gaming nooks

And quarter crannies

And cocktail hostesses tempting

A stupid man to leave a wife for

These aren't any ordinary

Donut dollies

They are royal princesses of voyeur pleasure

They don't look at me

Unless I'm at that one moment

When money floats down the whisky river

Close enough to the shoreline

They can bend over

Pick some up

Without getting their skimpy bathing suit

Uniforms wet.

But I got Dorothy's two hundred dollar shoes

In my hand

I've been wearing the same clothes

Since I got off the plane

My new suit

She's saving for

Valentines' Day dinner

Back in Portland.

I ask the security guard

Where in the hell am I

And is this a one-way street?

Over the helmeted heads

Of the cadre of coin cadets

Formation following close order drill

Marching towards the enemy

Of selfish fortune

Singing the battle hymn of tin

Clanging

Dropping leaflets of surrender or die

To a select few

Warriors of denial

He points past reproduced

Venetian art and European columns

Supporting

The illusion and elevators

Hovering people

From states as flat

As my bank account

Over the promise and surprise

Of lady luck.

She's crafty, wicked

Fucking smart

And very expensive.

I buy, she flies.

I make it to the room

Exchange shoes

I have to carry the open heeled

Ones' back across the

Shifting sands

Making maps useless

She stands there

The better part of an hour

And in Las Vegas that time

Is never well spent

Save the one-in-a-million lucky one: pardoned

And paroled from life as we know it.

I rescue my wounded companion

With rubber and leather slippers

To protect her tiny feet

From the scorch and torture

Of desert concrete.

Honking cabs, flashing bulbs

Japanese, Chinese, Asians

Porters and potters, limos and strollers

Waiting for the green light

To cross the street of anything.

Silly, silent and strong

The movement of her disposition

Changes everything

Bad to good

She makes me happy

When she takes my hand in hers

Steven G. Deaton

Funny thing about this

Vegas virga

It's raining all the time

In the desert oasis of love

But the water

Never really falls

On the ground.

Damn, Damn, Woman

Let's get

Right down to it.

It's always

The baggage; the unpacking

The repacking

What to leave behind

What to carry on

What to stay involved with

What to sever ties from

What to enliven and enrich

What to argue and to bitch

About

Our

Lives are complicated enough

Letters, phone calls, memories

And dreams

Fulfilled and the ones

Yet to be realized

Without you and with you

This

Aircraft does not have

An autopilot system

It's the superhero dream

Where the quiet sleeper

Is awakened

By the terrified scream

"Is anyone here a Doctor?"

Or

"Can anyone fly this plane?"

One of us has to get

Up and do something

Fast

Like lie a little to the passengers

First we throw the luggage out

I'll resuscitate the pilot

If you control the climb, cruise

And descent

'Cause damit, Woman,

Every take-off

Must equal one landing.

1979

Some Woman's phone number

Written

On the back

Of a cash register receipt.

Makes me think

Of all the times

In my life

I've cut myself

Shaving

And had to stop

And think

Of what it was

I was doing with

Some woman's phone number

Written

On the back

Of a cash register receipt.

One Mystery Solved

After re-uniting with my

On-again off-again Madonna

She asked me if I know

Or remember Yolanda

I drew a blank stare.

And, of course, said no.

It seems, she said, I tried to get

Her phone number and a little more

The first time Madonna

Was off-again.

Yolanda was clubbing with her

Friend Showeena.

Showeena, turns out, had seen a

Picture of me standing by my

On-again.

Now that picture had to be

A couple of years old even then

And no bigger then a Polaroid

A lot of me has changed with time

Which means

My little head

Couldn't have been the size of a dime.

Showeena

Picks up on my most serious lines

Across town

In a darkened bar

Places my face in the photograph

Whispers

Into Yolonda's ear

And that ended that fight

Way before last call.

Then Monday next

The woman they talk

And talk

Across the desk with my

Framed picture on it.

More than fourteen years later

And happy hours galore

My on-again Madonna

Tells me Yolonda was married

Tried to tell me no

But I kept pushing

Bartering for her soul.

It's embarrassing I say

I don't remember isn't enough

But now she knows

I know she knows

And now I see

What happens to me

When mixed with

Eight cubes of immoral agitation

Seven shakes of agnostic articulation

Six stirs of narcissist pacification

Five ounces of testosterone frustration

Four parts cavalier personification

Three shots of animated penetration

And

One-Two

Many Spanish coffees.

Out to Play

Twenty-four years

Or more

Yearning for my distant dream

Running

Out a back door life

Of a lovers

Drifting scream

Watching children out to play

Wondering what to be

Hoping they don't

Learn to grow

And live their life

Like me.

(1974)

Seventy-Two in the Light, Fifty in the Snow

There's a winter

Mountain range between us,

And

One hundred and ninety-eight miles

Of father and son pavement.

That's the closest

We've been

Since I don't know when

I think

It was the Army

When he drove me

To the induction station

Quiet

The whole trip

L.A. basin

Freeway interchanges

Cursing merging traffic

Cigarette in one hand

Coffee cup in the other

The radio playing

Merle, Johnny, Hank,

Their songs

Are all about whiskey

And the woman

That done them wrong, the dog that won't hunt

The fishin' boat that won't float

And the truck that won't start

Just when the repo men are comin' up the road

The taxman, the divorce attorney

And the second cousin with more bra then brains

Cause'n quite the family disturbance

At all the NASCAR races

The boss that won't let you go

The sheriff that didn't drive you home

Even though

He's your wife's sisters best friends in-law

Date'n your brothers

Daughter

And the guy that's raisin someone else's children

Just to sleep with his ex-problems

Seemed oddly out of place

In the steel casket

Me being carried towards

A certain helicopter death

With no lyrical background to speak of

And him

Driving

Away from an argument

With his wife

My mother

"Don't let our son go," she cried

Some thirty years ago.

Damn if he was right

Now I know

Whatever the fuck freedom

I fought for

Was short lived

And strangely intense

He's fighting for his life now

At Seventy-two in God's light

And

I'm driving

With another girlfriend

Hoping this one works out

Over those cold mountains

To see him

Radio playing

Merle, Hank, and Johnny

Me with a cigarette

In one hand

And a coffee cup in the other

Whispering the words

To those songs

Doing fifty in the snow.

Steven G. Deaton

The Deceitful Tactic of Keeping Him Guessing

It's the female voice

That asks the first question

A man's got

To stay on his toes.

Whether lies

Short stories

Or

Incomplete sentences

Respond

With reassuring hugs

And gentle kisses.

Trust me

Stay true

To the masculine gender

Avoid

Direct eye contact

Never let her

Position herself

Between you and the door

Least you need

To get past her

'Cause Lord knows how

She

Already has the answer.

The Night Someone Was Waiting for Joe

Joe McHenry, the only black guy pilot

In the Oregon Army National Guard

Drove me home early

One day

After a flight

We carpooled to and from Salem

To save gas.

He wouldn't come in for coffee

Said he had someone waiting

For him at home.

So I found my own way in.

My gun was hanging in the closet

Beside the bed

Where I found them

Her cameraman and my producer wife

Fucking to beat the

Lead story

Hoping to get the

Exclusive scoop.

I have pointed a pistol

At smarter guys then him,

And her

And cocked back the hammer

Without a chance at loosing sleep

Over the thought of

Divorce or death, or profession.

I had to think a minute.

In Los Angeles, the police call

Themselves SWAT.

Special Weapons and Tactics.

In Oregon, In Portland,

We take a softer approach to crime.

SERT.

Special Emergency Response Team.

Same shit, different city, different people

Same shit.

Barricaded felons, hostage takers, terrorists,

And just plain old' fuck ups.

I am a member of a

Special Emergency Response Team

Now more important than marriage

And ever.

I look for the gun.

They, the two of them,

Fumble for clothes and excuses.

I just want to make sure

They don't kill themselves,

Or me.

I turn around with the gun

Put it in the trunk of my car

And take the long liquid way over to

The girl I know I have loved

From the first time I saw her

At the police academy.

"What's wrong?" She asks. "You have

never come over like this before!"

"Oh, I'll tell you later, but I'm drunk now

Just let me stay over tonight, I'll

Take you out to dinner tomorrow."

"Sleep on the couch"

I unloaded my conscience

In a pathetic

Self-absorbed fashion

Placed my bullets

On the coffee table

Of my future love

And wondered if

Joe McHenry made it home OK.

The Reperception of Circadian Rhythm

"There is a procedure in every part of nature that is perfectly regular and geometrical if we can but find it out."

—John Woodward (1699)

Monday, I was half asleep when the bedroom door pushed open. A thin, faceless man, could have been me, came into the room and stood beside my bed. I was too tired to get up, yet my eyes were open and I could understand and feel his presence. In that single moment, I was not afraid for myself. This man waved his hand over my face several times until my vision became dull. I tried to get up, to be with him, but I seemed to be held in place by my own unnatural discord.

"Bill, someone is at the door." Pat said.

"I'm busy right now, can't you get it?" That question came in from another room.

Pat walked from the kitchen silently cursing her husband for not answering the door. He is always busy, she thought. He never answers the door. The doorbell rang again.

"Get the door!" Bill yelled.

Pat opened the front door. A young man was impatiently leaning against a porch beam.

"A telegram for Mr. And Mrs. Williams, sign here." He said.

"Oh, Okay." Pat answered.

She took the telegram, turned and walked back into the kitchen. She set it on the breakfast table, and then looked out the window viewing the back yard.

"That son-of-a-bitch Williams is always getting us into some sort of voluntary situation which spells only trouble." I said. "Are your guns loaded?"

"Yes sir," answered the door gunner, "good to go."

"Alright then, keep your eyes and ears open." I switched my radio mic from intercom to transmit.

"Centaur two-eight, this is Rescue eight-zero, over."

"This is two-eight, go ahead."

"We are in the air with an E.T.A. of one-zero minutes, over."

It was an unusually quiet morning. There was a thin layer of fog lying close to the ground that stretched from village to valley to rice paddy. From the air it looked as if someone spread a beautiful white blanket across the countryside, but left the treetops uncovered.

"Roger," answered two-eight, "We are under heavy ground attack, suggest south-west entry into the firebase. Hurry, I don't think we can hold our position much longer."

"Copy, south-west. Hold on Captain, I'll get you out."

On the horizon, I could see the bombs exploding on the firebase. There were bright flashes of fire through the early morning fog. If a tree fell over on a deserted island, would it make any sound? As I started descending into the war and the fog, I realized that if you concentrate on someone, you can hear everything or nothing.

"What makes you happy, Steve?" Barbara asked.

That was a stupid fucking question, I thought. I could lie to her by saying all those things women want to hear, like love, like her, like this thing we're doing. But, I didn't. I got out of bed and walked over to her dresser. She must have had every type of perfume manufactured to win the battle of the sexes. They were all lined up like tin soldiers, faceless ones, each fighting for the right to conquer one certain kind of man. I started to read some of the labels then looked at her behind me in the mirror. God, she was beautiful, lying there under a white blanket, warring in a half-loved stupor, just wounded, legs uncovered.

"Pretending to be sane." I said.

"What was that?"

"It makes me happy; pretending to be sane."

I looked at the clock on the dresser top. It was 1:45.

Sometimes when I dream, I believe the experience is really happening. Some of the colors are so vivid and sometimes just stark black and white, but real nonetheless. I was sitting in the classroom staring at my desk. The instructor had just passed out our mid-term exams. While everyone in the class was writing, the lights in the ceiling started falling on the desks. No one moved. They just kept writing. They didn't even flinch. One light fell right on top of my paper. I leaned over the desk and started spitting glass out of my mouth. When I realized what was happening, I was off the bed sideways spitting on the bedroom floor, tangled up in a white blanket, and Barbara was just out of reach.

Bill walked into the kitchen. He saw the telegram on the table.

"Who was at the door?" He asked.

Pat moves towards another time, almost out of reach of Bill, and just as quietly she returns.

"There was a nice young man, impatient though. He looked a lot like Steve did when he was younger. He brought us a telegram."

Bill sat down and opened the envelope.

Dear Mr. And Mrs. Williams:

We regret to inform you that your son, Captain Steven Williams, was killed in action while flying in a U.S. Army helicopter engaged in a combat rescue mission in Quang Tri Province, Republic of South Vietnam, Monday, September 9, 1972, 1:45pm.

"Would you like some more coffee?" The waitress asked.

"Just a half-a-cup, thanks." I said.

Every time I sit in one of these campus coffee houses with Barbara, I always start to feel smart. Last time I met her here we started talking about self-determination and the war. She doesn't believe in free choice. The war, to her, has always been non-existent; like a tree falling on a deserted island, she would never hear it. I stared across the table at her while she sipped her coffee. I knew I would marry her without even asking and I knew it would never last without a death.

"What are you thinking about?" I asked.

"Circadian Rhythm." She answered. "It is a biological time-measuring system. Are you familiar with it?"

"Well no, not really. Tell me something about it."

"Well," she explained, "first you must consider the activity patterns of animals with respect to a twenty-four hour cycle; when they eat, when they sleep, reproduce, you know, the light-dark thing and when they die. It can get pretty complicated."

"Yeah, go on."

"These animal rhythmic and time-dependent activities surely occur in man, but not in such extreme form as in the many creatures of the wild. You know, man's self-ordained difference, we wear watches; it screws us all up.

We never listen to or we can't hear our own selves think unless we look at a clock. How are we to respond to our own natural needs? Anyway, most of the circadian studies have been on plants and insects, and birds. You know, their migrations and navigation patterns. It's fascinating, really."

I nodded, lit a cigarette then signaled for a warm up.

"Why," she continued, "If we could really understand and control our activity patterns of rhythmic change, we would be less concerned about any variations of our environment. We would fly south for the winter and north for the summer."

She started to smile.

"It's just a matter of understanding timing. Timing systems, within, are clearly examples of regularity as well."

I can feel her. Her warmth. I can touch her. Her mouth, her lips, her hair. She is as perfect for this moment as any timing system could produce. She is the light and the dark in me and I am the summer and the winter in her. And the trees are falling all around me and she can't hear them.

"Oh look!" she started. "It's late, it's 1:45. I have to get up in the morning. I have to go. Do you think it will be foggy tomorrow? I hate the fog, can't concentrate on any thing; it's scary. Will you pick me up if it is, you know, foggy?"

I landed the helicopter just inside the firebase, light on the skids, ready to take-off.

"Go, Go, Go, get Captain Williams!" I yelled.

The gunner released the trigger on the machine gun and jumped out. What seemed like minutes were just passing seconds. Williams was shot in the leg. The gunner grabbed him and carried him back to the helicopter. There was enemy machine gun fire on us. The bullets were striking the tail of the aircraft. The gunner threw him on the floor, jumped on, I pulled pitch and we were airborne. As I banked the aircraft south, we took several more direct hits. The gunner had been shot in the head and was hanging by the safety straps around his machine gun mount. Captain Williams was also shot again and dead. The wind, the fog, the trees exploding and the queer quiet dulled my vision.

I reached for the white blanket, pulled it over my legs. My head rested on the pillow and the man stopped. He didn't walk out or move away, he was just gone. In his place, beside my bed, was a mirror. I stared into the mirror for a long time before I woke up. I kicked the blanket off, got out of bed and walked to the dresser. I fumbled around the top for a cigarette, knocking over some bottles of perfume. She was behind me in the mirror, beautiful, half asleep, warring with peace. I glanced at her clock.

35

Steven G. Deaton

On a Need to Know Basis

We are revered

In relatively small circles

Save the uncommon few

But what's all the way out there?

None of my friends

Even knew.

A lot of them tried to tell me

But I don't trust

Anything but my gut.

I turned to the

Federal Government

For some answers

For some trust

Before they can tell me anything

They needed a sample

Of my stool.

That's not what I trusted

I tell them

But secret secrets are their

Lies

And the common good truth

Is their capitol disguise.

You play the game

With them

Or the answer you seek will never

Materialize.

I need a secret clearance

For them to analyize.

So I gave them one

The best I could produce

They sent it to a lab of theirs

And mailed me the report.

My world is smaller now,

Seems the

Son-of-a-bitch fry cook

That gave me gas

Had shared an intimate part

Of my ex-wife's

Past.

Say When

Just say when:

When are you coming home?

When are you going to call?

When do you have to be at work?

When will I see you again?

When are you coming over?

When are you going to finish what you started?

When are you going to take out the trash?

When will you call your mother?

When can I expect the money?

When is enough enough?

When will it ever be right?

When will this madness end?

When will the debits end and the

Credits begin?

When will I be discovered?

When will it go on sale?

When do I have to pay?

When are they arriving?

When did you do that?

When did I say that?

When did you go there?

When did they tear that down?

When did they choose sides?

When did he call?

When did she call?

When did they leave?

When can I start?

When can I stop?

When did you say it would happen?

When will I ever be happy?

When did they build that?

When did they put that there?

When did you see me?

When will I ever learn?

When will you be eighteen?

When is summer?

When are the fireworks?

When do the ships come in?

When are you coming to bed?

When are we going to eat?

When are we going to get there?

When are you going to grow up?

When will you know?

When is it due?

When is the right time?

When are you going to marry me?

When are you going to divorce her?

When are you going to meet my parents?

When are you going to tell them?

When did this happen?

When did I get old?

When are the midterms?

When will I see the light?

When is the court date?

When is the announcement?

When were you going to tell me the truth?

When did I gain this weight?

When did I lose the receipt?

When have I ever been wrong?

When was the accident?

When does the show start?

When are you leaving?

When is the execution?

When did you meet?

When are you available?

When is it over?

When is it going to be OK?

When did you call?

When is it my turn?

When did you know it was right for you?

When are you ever going to listen?

When will you ever understand?

When will I ever be loved?

When do I hold, when do I fold?

When did you change?

When are you going to let it go?

When can I ever get some sleep?

When are you going to come clean?

When do we have to get up?

When did you say they were coming?

When does the liquor store close?

When does the bank open?

When have you ever been there for me?

When is the car fixed?

When have you ever been right?

When are you going to make a commitment?

When were you born?

When is the funeral gonna be?

When will you learn the world does not revolve

Around you?

D. Elizabeth LaClair

Steven G. Deaton

Silk Roses

Vinyl

Turkey ham

Eggbeaters

Diet coke

Nogahide

Imitation leather

Nutri-sweet

Near beer

Miracle whip

Ice milk

Your shit don't stink

Rest rooms

Moving sidewalk

Stationary bike

Plastic ivy

Poisoned love

Transvestites

Domestic partner

Test tube babies

Music television

Mini-van

The Delorean

Spruce goose

Temporary insanity

Induced labor

Cubic zirconium

Silicone

Krab meat

Boca burger

Cheese whiz

Cool whip

Substitute teacher

Surrogate mother

Artificial horizon

IQ test

Foster homes

Climate control

Instant winner

Padded bras

Falsies

Penal implants

Blow-up dolls

Dildos

Presto logs

Books on tape

Clearance sale

Day old bread

Waterless soap

Lifetime guarantee

Homeowner

Miniature golf

Zoos

Astro-turf

Tinted windows

Stained glass

Electoral college

Mid-life crisis

Energy saver

One-size fits all

Censorship

Divorce attorney

Dry cleaning

Sensitivity training

Retreats

Legalized drugs

Fun in the sun

Tanning booths

Sunscreen

Designer knock-offs

Virtual reality

Fake-ID

Loopholes

Buy now, save money

Decaf coffee

Virgin cocktails

Glass eye

Smokeless tobacco

Faux furs

Faux pearls

Wigs

Viagra

Prozac

Marriage license

Shaving

Equal opportunity

Upper-middle class

Four wheel drive

Phone sex

Instant credit

Credit same as cash

Rentown

All you can eat

Free refills

Buy one get one free

Computer enhanced

Voice over

Veneer

False teeth

Las Vegas

Lip synch

National Enquirer

Entertainment tonight

Diversity training

Singles clubs

No Doze

Nite all

Liquid fabric

Biodegradable refuge

Bacon bits

Day light savings time

DWCF athletic body younger than my 40 plus years

Seeks S/DBM 42 plus, age not important, some children OK

Lite smoker

Social drinker who enjoys long walks on the beach

Quiet evenings by the fire, disco, reading, movies, country drives

Bungee jumping, horseback riding, collecting butterflies, looking for travel and companionship, must be financially secure and not afraid of exploratory sex, maybe something further.

Must like my four children and favor friendship with my ex.

If you're that man send picture.

No games please.

The Immeasurable Distance Between You and Me

"Has the notion of suicide

ever entered your thoughts?"

The veteran's psychiatrist

Posed that question

During my separation interview.

"No, not ever."

In truth

I had lied about college credits

Enough for pilot training

Had a history of failed relationships

My first ran away from home unnoticed

Much to the awful surprise

Of her parents and me

On a school night.

The second

Couldn't support the war in Vietnam

And I remember

Being crouched behind a tree

Breathing hard

Watching

The beads of sweat

Splashing down off my face

Onto the cylinder

Of the .38 caliber special revolver

In my right hand

My left hand

Was calculating the longevity

Of my time remaining

On this planet

By feeling for the stored bullets

On my pistol belt.

My minds eye counted ten left;

Not much time.

I raised my stare

From the sweaty revolver

To the trail behind me

I see way the fuck more

Then ten single shot North Vietnamese regulars

Celebrating

The Tet offensive of nineteen hundred seventy-two

Each with a machine gun

Each committed to claiming their trophy: me.

I was being hunted as food for the war machine.

At twenty-one

I stood up from behind that tree

As methodical and disappointed

As an old man does

When he knows the fish aren't going to bite

Anymore

And it's time to go home alone.

I turned and aimed

Sent six last supper invitations

Down that trail

As if I addressed each one personally.

What I got back

Was rapid fire RSVP's

And a few last chance offers myself.

A few of the enemy rounds

Hit my self-esteem

One or two wounded my pride.

I reloaded the remaining four

And random fired

Three dear occupant invitations

To join me.

Not a single bullet

Slowed their rush to the banquet.

I thought about

Dropping the gun.

But I had a foreboding notion

To keep

A self-addressed

VIP escort

Under the hammer

I holstered the pistol

Swallowed my wounded pride

Fucked the remaining self-esteem

Turned and ran to high heaven.

Hungry or not

I decided to be late for their dinner

Then and there

I began my starvation diet.

Just like an excited boy

Innocence lost

Running out the back door

When the young girls

Father is coming in the front

I was half euphoric, half scared.

From that exact moment on

I am always running

To the tree line

To see if

Another helicopter will save me.

I am a hunter now

I have run through fields

Of stone and flowers

Trying to track down

And kill the bastards

That hunt me restless and reckless.

I have been prey

To emotional hardships

And irresponsible timing

I have cleverly trapped

Honesty and fairness

Turned their souls to deception

Only to be wounded

By my own steel teeth.

There is no tomorrow

There is no such thing as a slow run.

There is just the twenty-four hour a day

Rush to escape the temptation

To ride the dragon escort

To a lesser communion with God.

I had decided

Intimacy was a slower suicide

And ran

I drink too much

I smoke too much

I eat too much

I love too little

Until now, until you.

My body, your body

Is the temple Christ

Chose to hide the suicide

Serpent.

Need it, feel it, praise it

Celebrate it

Live it, but don't waste it.

Feed it

Feed it with kindness, companionship,

Love and food.

Good food.

I think you, like Christ

Is a gatherer.

I cannot be a gatherer

Unless I drop the gun.

Hunters, like me

Are always looking for something

Other than what was

Gathered for them from the beginning:

Food for the natural order of things; love.

My last straw

Of misfortune

Will be my own misunderstanding.

I am situated

Behind the trees

Exactly as you are.

Let's stand up

With the poise and confidence and inspiration

Of life and love

Realize the trail behind us

Is shorter than the path ahead.

Instead of beginning a starvation diet

Let's simply embrace

The moment's nourishment

Turn and walk

From now until all the tomorrows

I watch the same sunset

You do.

I stood up with shaky confidence

Took a deep breath of composure

Realized God was on their side

And mine

Without jurisprudence or malice

I was thinking of validating my own travel plans

To higher ground

When the knock on the door

Sounded like I wasted nine shots

I hoped it was you

I answered

It was you.

End the hunger pains

Feed me.

To Steal a Pilot from a Plane

The invitation reads:

This may be the last time

We will be together again.

I placed one in the highest cloud

For the sun to see.

I set one in the wind

For Mother Nature to read.

I wrote another

Above the sea

So there can never ever be

A doubtful reason why

My heart was taken from the sky.

I met a woman

The notation said

She laid one on my billowy bed

She is everything good

I see in each of you

She's the stars

That celebrates a moonless night

She's the clouds

That play to heavens delight

She is the wind and the sun

The storm and the calm

She is the purpose

Of every season

From this flight on.

I've questioned her deception

I'm stationed for her resolve

Her guard is her attraction

Her glory her distress

Death is now my mistress

My abandon and my name.

She is the only woman

I know of

To steal a pilot from a plane.

May 17, 2001

Steven G. Deaton

Maria's Entrance

Finally the entrance I was sentry for.

From the ladies room to my bar stool

I estimate her rate-of-closure to be

Two feet per second I stand to block

Her martini destination.

She looks up at me with eyes sultry mixed

Bacall without the signature cigarette

Weaver facing off the Alien Three.

And dressed like, different, like a real woman.

The kind of woman who laughs at a man

Who doesn't appreciate a subtle mystery?

Restless streams, a first full moon rising

Between the glass and steel glitter and gold

Of downtown doorways leading nowhere

But up and down the sliding scales of life.

Dogs growl to protect her

Cats play to amuse her

Horns bark, strings meow as light

Dinner jazz lays red carpet at her feet

She moves and the wind changes direction.

The Chairman of the Board himself

Could have praised the future in song

If she sipped champagne

In the back of his airplane.

Even dreamers sing "fly me to the moon,

Let me live among the stars'

You know, that kind of real woman,

Different.

Maria's Constellation

The western red in the sunset skies

Thinks the eastern stars a jealous notion

To steal the bright sparkle from your eyes

With help of the wind from the Pacific Ocean.

The young trees bend and the old leaves flow

Within the giggle of the evening rustle

Cause it's the love you send they know they show

And not that silly Atlantic potion.

The gentle sun and all the stars in between

The ones to be heard and want to be seen

All move and wonder with fascination,

Where were you when they were young

Still learning the name of your constellation?

The Portland moon has the right lovely notion

For this curious heavenly potion

The Pacific wind her immaculate consumption

To move the blue shadows from your night

So God will sleep knowing

You live in his light.

Maria's Exit

I have a picture of her

Standing in the kitchen

Holding a bottle of wine

Italian red table dry,

Chianti.

Polite nose, poised palate

Conversation encouraged, crafty

Old oak bouquet, rich color

Deep anticipation, higher expectations

Lofty goals, earthy flavor

Hand picked, skillful assortment

Vintage year, bottle corked

Low light, temperate humidity

Basement stored, not off the rack

Smoky hints of complex intuitions

And subtle suggestions of quiet resolve

Expensive label, affordable bottle

To the right debt to income ratio.

She was married to an Italian poker player

Who tried to keep the wine in the cooler

Of extra-matrimonial bravado.

Half drunk

Expecting the flavor to stay young

With bigger game, higher stakes.

I never met an Italian American,

Save one in Colorado,

That knew substance over style, anyway

And so it goes,

She was uncorked and shelved

In the Kenmore of relationships

Refrigerated light

Her children opening the door

Warm air rushing in

Cold air rushing out

Hands reaching past for food

Anything to eat

Little compassion mostly compulsion

To stoke the fires of youth

And scatter the coals of burning amber

The greasy card shark found a fresher deck to cut.

I'm a gambler of sorts, so is she.

I bet to lose, she never bluffs

Anymore

She's a woman acting

Hell bent on overcoming stage freight

For herself this time.

So it goes wrong

At first, then it's the right thing

At last.

I have a picture of Maria

Standing in the kitchen.

I tried to take one of her

In the living room

But it didn't develop right

Overexposed with cautious determination

To rid the red wine

Of equally committed

Impurities and free radicals

Unnatural light Dark shadows

Not an effortless Kodak pose

Photography is

The telling tale for actors, actresses, extras

And such

Critics say

The camera loves the good ones

The real people

Not much.

O' Poetry Corner

The sixth day of the week I wonder

Why in the world would you print that blunder

Of English lit and superfluous grit

In your school of composition, I slumber.

The sleepy words of the pedigree poets

Don't make up for the recognition bestowed

From paper editors who with charm

And middle school wit

Couldn't find milk

In a dairy cow's……

It's not the cream of the word crop

In Saturday's print

It's not the answer to life's bewilderment.

It's never the teacher but the student with the answer.

The staff and the managers all agree

The Oregonian plainly must be

Not to the left and never right

Cause office chairs are designed

To encourage the fear of heights.

If you turn in small circles on top of the world

South is in every direction

If you believe that you can't go wrong

Save your retirement, you need protection.

Words were never meant to humble the meek

It's the strength of poetry the General's seek

To liberate the oil from the madman's soil

What a General can do with words to convince

An Army to triumph over insolence.

There is no superman under Clark Kent's clothes

He threatens our minds with the poetry of doles.

We must find the evildoer with the reporter's front

And shine a light in his crypt to night.

Like front page news on the seventh day,

Every battle has its price to pay

His words were weak but the message alive

Gore says salmon must survive.

Come on, My God, make passions hotter

Stand up, Stand up, dare to speak louder.

My father says the son of his son's war will be fought

Not for oil but for water.

Steven G. Deaton

Without a body we have nothing

Two young men

Held seven women captive

In a bar

At gun point

For a night and a day.

While police stood outside

And waited

Round the barricade.

Six O'clock News reports

Wine and women

Carried them to their graves.

Dallas Cowboys six

Miami Dolphins zero

Good evening, we're glad you joined us

Your news center team

Looking out for you

Jim, Tom, Ann, Mat and Dan

Katie and the cameras are live

For reports on the fives.

Later in the program

We'll talk to an expert

On raising your children

Do you like me so far?

Back in a moment

You need a new car.

Steven G. Deaton

The Quiet Night Disturbed

I tried to call to you

But I cannot.

I reach for the phone

But never can touch

It moves backwards

Across the thin space

From deep in the oceans of cracks

In the air you are gone. Snap.

Process. Equip the mind

To turn off the geyser

Of melted snow

And reach for the ice instead

It will burn at first

But it has not yet turned to water

And will last as long as you, as I,

Can stay cool.

There is something powerful determined

Desperate to hear your own siren wail

Wake up sleepy blocks

Through suspect neighborhoods

Announce the second coming

Of the battle civil disturbance

Not to be awakened giants of complete doom

Not yet anyway

I can handle it, let me pass

Through the quiet night disturbed.

Trust me, go back to sleep rest

I will hunt the human beast down for trespass

And end it for you:

Good night my sweet dreams of adventure

And romance. In the morning sun

I will drink from the rain

Collected for you

To you and what could have been had we met

In your slumber colors and what is now

Will never be again

Black and white. Reload.

I call to someone like before; get the notes

Of some young girl

Waiting for a chance to prove

Her innocence in a nasty way.

It is my turn to be like you.

To be with you.

Just let me touch your face

I will not stay too long.

Come to me the quiet night. Leave my head

On your pillow of doubtless dreams

Not to hear desperate talk

Of rueful schemes

And drowning sirens of silent screams

Come to me the quiet night.

Let my siren call

Rustle with the horrible fright.

I'm no prize husband

My wife of five years

Confessed everything to me on our honeymoon.

She smoked Kool cigarettes up until the time we met,

She dropped acid with a paroled felon

On a regular basis

And fucked in the grass under the sun burnt trees

During and after the Friday night football game

In the evening Pacific breeze

In the only park outside

Downtown Lodi California.

Everybody did it; it's what you do in Lodi;

Just to piss your mother off.

He had bad teeth she told me

She felt sorry for him and

While she worked as a motel housekeeper

Near Interstate five

While attending junior college

With traveling men older than me

Hitting on her for a feel and you know

What else because what attracted me to her

In the first place were her breasts;

She paid for his new teeth.

She was nineteen, I understood the way

Her sweaters fit.

I didn't know she was nineteen until our

Second date when she asked me if I would buy

Her and her roommates some beer.

After she was drunk she asked me on the porch

If I was ever going to kiss her.

She graduated four A's and a B plus

Me straight C's except the D in sociology

And the incomplete psychology.

We eloped to Carson City Nevada.

Funny thing. Little did I know that

My parents, Bill and Pat, married in Carson City,

Back in forty-eight.

I thought I had normal teenage dated;

My dad drove me to my first dance.

Her father committed suicide

When her mother was so excited with her news.

I wish I knew my parents better.

They have been together for over fifty years now

Still going strong and he even e-mails all his children.

Five kids, all modest, one poor, one rich.

All have children, mostly daughters, except me.

I chose not to procreate with my wife of five years.

From our blissful matrimonial bed until

The time we split

It was who could out fuck who

Without fucking each other.

I stayed poor and we ended up

Fucking each other good.

She claimed she was pregnant several times

And I said to her, as

I saw the words coming out of my mouth

And I couldn't stop them

They came out so damaging and dislocated,

"I want no children of mine to have you as their mother"

and that started our five year relationship

with the Portland Free Clinic.

I figure her to could have

Single handedly increased the planet's population

Two fold.

If not in practice, in theory.

A friend at the time, another policeman, told me:

If she had as many pricks sticking out of her

As she had sticking in her

She'd be a porcupine.

Looking back, it was his way of saying

He could be a father to any of my wife of five years' children.

My decision to divorce her was made on our wedding night

During her confession.

I acted on that decision five years later.

That's my way;

Put everything off until the last minute.

I think the reason she confessed

Is because I was a policeman.

And I'm not a policeman anymore

Because of her, not him, or him, or him

Or him, or……

Sometimes the most sincere confessions

Can be misunderstood and confused

With the rules and regulations

Of honest remorse.

I wasn't always patrolling quiet streets.

Loud and strong were my tactics

Smooth and sure was my modus operandi.

Many a nights I pointed the pistol to arrest

Innocent girls trying to prove their mother's wrong,

Then released the prisoners via back seat bail.

A select few I wished I'd married

Some I wish I knew

Most I hope to remember

Others I forget

One or two I thought I saw a child.

Not now not ever

I'm no male prize;

I can live with that.

Right now I'm righteous

Like my wife of five years would say

Steve, There's a woman out there

That's just right for you.

I pray in my old age

She is not her again.

Steven G. Deaton

I Haven't Told You The Good News Yet

I'm not that attractive

Anymore

I smoke cigarettes

Taught when it was cool

I drink wine

Cold or room temperature

Learned that in the dorm

I drink whisky

Cold or room temperature

Army schooled, Irish encouraged

I drink coke-a cola

Without ice

Southeastern Asian trick

I drink coffee

No cream, no sugar

Black

Too many Arabian nights

I drink water

Out of the tap

Just can't forget what's free

I drink Knudsen's cherry fruit drinks

I did when I was young,

It seemed to work

I drink seven-up

With two aspirin

It's on the pre-flight checklist

I drink some beer

If it's the only thing left

In the refrigerator

I drink kool-aid

At hospitals

Stay away from Gatorade, Jones soda, orange juice and

Milk

No matter how hard you try,

That glue don't stick

I drink lemon aide

Rarely

I drink tea

With Chinese

I drink scotch

Happy hour whenever

On Saturdays

I drink wine

I already said that

But I didn't mention why

I drink wine

During the week when

I've been heard to slur my words

And bump into low furniture

I feel I'm not attractive anymore

And I have to smoke a cigarette

To contemplate

My fall from grace

With members

Of the opposite sex.

I'd like to think it was

A gradual decline

And I enjoyed the slow descent

Rather than an all-of-a-sudden

Steep declination

Of female interest

Cause the slide on the slippery slope

Won't kill you

It's the irrevocable stop

At the end

That worries me.

She Rights Herself

I want to see the news program

On the occasion of my birthday.

Before I drink too much

Playing with my present Dorothy.

Those crazy Floridians and their very public storms

The Christian, The Jew, The Texas Baptist

The career politician, it's hard to follow them

Save the constant coverage

To justify, to rectify, to certify, to simplify.

And on my fiftieth birthday I toast

To that.

If I can't finish what I started with her

She will curse the scotch the same way

Lightning rips the wind without confusing condemnation.

If I love her too much, she will simplify me.

If I love her too little, she will rectify me.

If I hurt her love, she will certify her own resolve.

If I choose to protect her, she will justify her independence parade.

It was that election on T.V.

That surprised me

When over debate so close to argument

She was without opinion and indifferent to a re-count.

Steven G. Deaton

Never in our publicity

Has she been passive to voice

Or better yet

Submissive to my oddball politics

Without awareness of her options.

Or else she has never lived in Florida

And is cooler then I first imagined.

Dorothy, I believe, like Christ must have believed

When he saw his disciples go in different directions

Each in order to be nearer to him, knows

That nature elects to play politics

With love and competition

Armed with options

Each to right herself without confusing condemnation.

Tender, down the Perfume River

The doctor was across the isle

Window seat nervous,

Looking out at the maturing

Cumulus Nimbus clouds talking

Non-stop to the woman worldly sexy

Poised by beauty and grace and dress, between us.

And I know the fragrance, Chanel Number Nineteen.

It is Pascale's intoxicating signature.

I want to hear her voice

But he won't stop listing his academia yidda yadda

Not a real doctor because he doesn't know

What ails us.

She is as politely disinterested in him

As was Pascale with me a couple of years ago.

But this woman's perfume lifts my fondest heart

Floats it gently through my rapid river

Of youth and yearning memories.

The woman would drive me wild

With interruptions towards the good doctor

If she were heard to be French.

Pascale did that to me forever

In the shortest amount of time,

She etched a template of love and beauty

In my mind hard now to draw on.

But this woman is composition by design,

Art by creation,

She has drawn my attention back to Pascale.

Then I would call her message machine

Just to hear her voice

Would stimulate the olfactory gland and

I could smell her even during the recording

"I will be out of the office until Wednesday"

And my eyes would water with Chanel Nineteen.

The doctor is an exhibit designer

For the museum at the University of Wisconsin.

This is his first trip to Portland

To meet with the artist

Try to exhibit his complicated sculptures.

The airplane and the clouds make him nervous.

I think the rabid mouth PhD can't know Art

Even if he walked up and slapped that silly grin off his face.

I am an artist

My brush the airplane

My canvas the sky.

In my time I have sacrificed everything for my art.

It's not that complicated, it's the sacrifice

That defines composition, composure

And presentation.

The real exhibit designer is stationed civility

Between us

And onto both of us.

I am delighted and the Doc hapless persistent.

She holds a beautifully bound book in her lap

Closed long fingers supporting a diamond

Worthy of sacrifice to the right gentleman

Announcing yet concealing her presentation,

Past and present situation,

From the likes of PhD's and me.

Him, it's a confinement and a obligatory introduction

Me, she already knows and yearns for a smooth landing

And ushered retreat.

Pascale was right all along

When she figured out I would take too long

Rest on too many excuses

Swipe my brush across the endless canvas too many times

Then she left me with the

Comfort only regret can embrace.

And the smell of her neck

When she turned her head away from my lips

Short quick gasps for air almost whispered cries

Damp humid clouds

Maturing holding everything in until

The right conditions fall water

Tender, down the Perfume River.

It runs west to east

Through the northern part of South Vietnam.

I've flown that watered sky before

Painted recklessness with nerve

Found heroism questioned with

A Cowardice hue

Forgave my own ambitious calls

Drowned my first dreams in red

There from my most saddened heart

My youthful love bled

Down the perfume river

Filling the South China Sea.

It's there that the French gave everything

And the Americans took all despair with defeat.

I was so small and thoughtless.

But like all the future artists,

I was confused by a bigger passion

Complicated by a simple love.

She surprised when she said

There, forget it, now you never have to go to France.

You have had everything in life

Paris has to offer.

Just like an American

You take and take and take and take

You never give and I must go

My desire is gone,

I must get it back.

If this commuter were bigger

Or the flight longer

She would move

When the seat belt sign was extinguished.

That's why time is important to composition and design

As well as creation and exhibition.

The doctor should shut up

And let us both enjoy the real exhibit designer

While the beauty in art lasts.

Steven G. Deaton

The Problem with Portland

I feel like

I'm falling towards pavement

Detached, drifting

Subject to the wind

Pauper to gravity

From cloud to ground

Prince to presumption

From corner to corner, street to block

Less strength than weakness

More loss than wins.

But water

When left alone

Finds it's own level

And in Portland

Where the snow melts down

The Cascades

Through forested parks

Past blocks of acceptance and denial

And streets of trial and error

One has to remember

Every turn for the worst

Lends gift to character, reflection to resolve

Distraction to attraction

Water to creeks

Creeks to streams

Streams to rivers

Rivers to oceans

Oceans to rain

I can stand on the city streets

Look left and right,

Look down

There are all my sacrifices

Mistakes and honors

In those gutter gates

Washing down towards

The Willamette River

North

To the confluence

Of the Columbia

Then West

To the mouth at the Pacific

Each time it rains

Returning to my feet

In every wet gray cloud

Borne from that ocean of romance

Hanging over Portland.

What the fuck, rain;

The love and the sorrow of it,

But it's only water.

That's why people can live here

Because

It is only water.

Washington, D.C.

I am a soldier still

Defending an unrelinquished soul.

Port arms, weary

Shoulders slumped

All I wanted to be

Was the victim of spoiled passion

On the battle playground

Of a young requited heart;

Aggressive to the end

Stomach in, chest out

Battles often end quickly

Wars haunt a lifetime.

Is it best to die young in a world

That will not forgive age?

The glory surrounds

The tomb of the unknown

Courage, honor, immortality lies quietly

Gracefully

And we try to remember

All there is to know.

Torment and pain

Are inscribed

Steven G. Deaton

On the monumental walls of war

To remind us we can never

Forget any of it.

Granite and marble scream

For what is put to rest with the child

Deceived by battles won

Wars are always lost

To the victim

In us all.

A Crisis Situation with a Win-Win Solution

Jesus said

Enough is enough

Something about a

Stone and throwing sin

Casting your soul away

I won't be the first

And never the last

The woman I married

Had more than

A

Colorful

Biblical past.

One night a week

Here

We meet for a day

There

I have to do this

She has to do

That.

But we are committed

For better

For worst

And that will be that.

So I go my way

She goes hers

I found several lovers

To match all

Of hers.

But the one I liked

Most of all

Couldn't possibly be

Any more gracious

Than the fruit

Of the forbidden tree.

She was everything

I wanted

But I couldn't see

Past the hardships

Of marriage

To the wrong woman who

Captured me.

Nothing I can say to her

Will ever

Forget

The right and the wrong of it,

My God,

This other woman

Set me free.

I left my wife

And a couple more

To live the good life

Hunting the

Troublesome whores

Okay, you thought

I was righteous

And I could forgive and forget

My own past

And the one

Of my pets

But let me tell you something

Least you never forget

The one that brought sin to you

Forever

Is the one that will live with you

Forever.

Steven G. Deaton

Belfast, N. Ire.

Low ceilings

In a basement pub

Lively

Irish heads

Bobbing in the drink

Neighborhood balladeers singing

Of wind swept sacrifices

And green green glory

I walk out the back door

Into an alley

Still laughing at their jokes

Bump into the barrel

Of a British soldier's

Last vestige of Royal Empire.

God Save The Queen,

I thought.

I dropped my cigarette

As he stepped back

Into the shadow of occupation.

With his eyes

I was directed away

From the street where

Two incinerated silhouettes

One behind the wheel

The other in the backseat

Lori still burning

Helicopter overhead

Constables directing chaos

Soldiers quiet in darkness.

If I would have stayed

For another round

I would have missed it.

That miniature siren scream

Of European police cars:

"To-do, To-do, To-do"

Not like we do it

In America.

The first thing you hear

Is the four-barrel carburetor kick in

Sucking Kuwaiti gold

We fought for it and won.

Thirsty never ever quenched

Our empire of consumption

Providence domain unchallenged

Unleashed, unbridled three hundred fifty V-8 horsepower

Claiming protection

Of persons, property, and liberty.

Siren commanding

"Now, Now, Now, Now."

Yea, America.

Not quiet, not hiding, up front.

"Lead, follow, or get out of the way."

Come to think of it

I did go back into that pub

For another round

Of Northern Ireland political fealty

Those brogue lads

Were so busy swimming in the stout

Titanic moored in leprechaun afterglow

Shout'n revolution slurring vengeance

"To-do, to-do"

In the Belfast enclave

They left the lovely, pale complexion

Lassies

Agitated

Stimulated

Unguarded.

Thus, any distraction

For prisoners of isles and lore

Whether domestic

Or on a foreign shore

Degrades the integrity of the captors

Encourages the resolve

Of the captive

And allows the unencumbered

Irish easy access.

"So yer stay'n at the Stormont?

Can I be drive'n yaw to the hotel?"

She asks.

My reply:

"Now, Now, Now".

Steven G. Deaton

Two Deluxe Cocktail Glasses
(Here's to Dorothy)

Do late night calls interrupt your mature sleep or just disturb your little girl dreams? Even Christopher Columbus, on his way to discovering a place, this place, where he thought no man had gone before was, historically, proved wrong. First of all, the Indians were already here, procreating, hunting and happy, and then there's proof that maybe a Scandinavian white man had already left some DNA in the forest of unknown borders, but Chris landed any way and immediately dispatched a message of discovery and understanding to his Queen. If he had a cell phone that roamed he would have called her. He was excited and unaware of any time zone differences of importance and consequence. No matter, she believed in him. Her King was suspicious. The Queen is in the envious position of always encouraging her Jacks and supporting her King. She plays them both well because without her, there is no royal connection. Her trouble has always been with the Ace, because the Ace can be played high or low, and can usually stand-alone. Or so she thinks. I'm an Ace. Sometimes I'm dreamer high or realist low. I have expectations never realized and dreams often dreamt and photographs of both to prove it. My logbook was stolen in Edmonton, Canada, right in the lobby of the downtown Hilton Hotel. I was having a drink in the mezzanine level overlooking the indoor garden and the tree branches came all the way up and touched the glass walls of the bar. High above the lobby the sun filtered thru stained glass skylights placed like nail holes breathing glory, down the inside balcony railings shinning like a cathedral and several shafts of light were engineered to illuminate the drink and the dream and hide the reality in the darkness below. I squinted. Hard to tell, but I couldn't see anybody praying for understanding and, of course, for forgiveness. I raised the glass; several glasses and ordered a salad. God is in this room I know it and we built glass from sand to keep his breath outside but the glass can't keep his eyes, the sun and the moon, from looking in on us even though the windows are to keep us from being closed in we really are closed out. It's the breath of fresh air that keeps peace with the planet, not the stained glass, it's brilliant. I placed an ad in the Edmonton Daily News about one quarter page size saying: "REWARD 500 DOLLARS U.S. NO QUESTIONS ASKED. Keep the luggage, Keep the change of clothes, Keep the shaving kit, and Keep the shoes and black socks. But PLEASE return the logbook. It means nothing but 500 dollars to you and everything else to me. Send SASE with logbook to me: Steven G. Deaton. 4202 NE 70TH Ave. Portland, Oregon, 97218. I will mail you a 500 dollar money order-No name-you fill it in and cash it." Any way, since then I stopped logging every hour away from home. That logbook was fifteen years of documenting a relationship of flight and understanding that exacted extreme sacrifices and modest rewards. I rely on memory and if my memory serves me right, like my earliest photos show, I can boldly state with authorization, provable authorization, that I am an Ace of sorts and have gone, on occasion, where no North American, Catholic, white man with two brothers and two sisters and parents who are still married to each other after fifty years and appear to be going for fifty more, although I am their only child they constantly worry about, has gone before. With enough conditions and qualifiers anyone can be a Ace of any kind and a Jack of all trades and if I had known you back then I would have used my cell phone, hell with the roaming charges and the exact time of day or night of the revelation and called you immediately after landing just to hear your voice and, confidentially, just to boast a little to camouflage the fact that I miss you terribly, our stares, our movie rentals, our talk, our classic music station kisses, warm to the lips, wet water beading, clinging, drying on starched shirts and spotting satin blouses unbuttoned and swelling, that either heats a cool night or quenches a pyromaniac passion intent on flame. You made me a matchstick that needs to have my cover closed before striking. I can live with a suspicious King, it means nothing to me, because a curious King is really only preoccupied with his own mortality and legacy. He has no time for discovery and understanding and thinks only of his Queen as frivolous and flighty. Not a doer, not even a teacher, but every thinking man needs a Queen somewhere near a cell site. I never got not even one response to my Canadian newspaper ad. I saved five hundred dollars but lost a chance at immortality of sorts. I was very depressed about the whole thing for a long time. Since then I have become preoccupied with understanding and with you. I know you still dream little girl dreams; rich princes, big palaces, exotic travel to undiscovered places, fine wardrobe envied by wives and mistresses alike, fresh and well prepared meals with old bittersweet wine. That's OK, because the dream once realized becomes the immortal one after all. A toast: to the woman in you that fires the furnace of a man's soul and to the little girl in you that bares passion naked of truth. I drink to you and to the wind and the clouds and to me and every chance I get I drink till I can see where it is that the stars end and I wonder why it is that we had to look so far away into the darkness of our lives to see the raised glass, the light and the glory of love. I'll drink to that and to you, and I understand the dream on Saturday and I'll pray for forgiveness on Sunday only if it gets me to Monday and another week of discovery. I dream I'm in a mayonnaise jar with a few nail holes in the lid and a twig and a piece of lettuce browning at my side. I haven't bathed since someone put me in here without my luggage and I'm on a shelf or something in a dark room could be a garage or shed somewhere in Columbus because only once in awhile I wake to see two eyes one as big as the sun the other the moon near the glass and the light must be an Indian summer and the shaking jar disturbs my sleep but my cell phone rings and the eyes and the hand put the jar down and turns out the light and slams the door to the garage or shed or whatever but the light of the cell phone window displays "call from Dorothy" and the glory of love shines through the nail holes and it's there that the stars end and the dream begins. I throw my Scandinavian wool sweater down I can use the twig to scale the glass walls to be near you when you come and twist the lid open I only have five hundred dollars on me but it's yours no questions asked what took us so long to answer each others ad. Hell, no one has ever seen a Canadian newspaper much less read one, I mean what could they print, a list of hiding places? What was I thinking anyway, the bastards; lettuce dream together.

I'm Right Here

Take a break

From loneliness…

Forever,

I love you.

You may think

That trick doesn't work

But it's a proven fact

After all is said

And done

I'm the one

Who screws the bolts

Into the nuts

That holds the hooks

That hangs the pictures

Of our families

On the walls

Of the room

In the house

With the kitchen and the one and a half baths

Aluminum siding

Paint chipping

Garden crying

Garage hiding

And the washer

And dryer

Lint free

Environmentally safe

Dishwasher

Vacuum cleaner extra bags

Safeway club card

Special savings to subscribers

Keep an eye on the oil prices

California wine

For the guests

French for the best

Nights

Extension cords

Half yearly sale

Don't forget the Sunday paper

One night a year

We'll use the good

China

Maybe talk about

Swimming in the Bahamas

Line the garbage can

Paper or plastic

What the fuck

Did we get ourselves into

Again

You've been through this before

With another man

Me another woman

I will never

Forget who I am

Or where I came from

And I will always

Love you for who you are.

I can't live in the past

And I don't plan the future

Past dawn

So don't worry

I'm right here.

I have it all

Figured out.

We can file

Separate or joint…

Jesus,

You turn me on.

Steven G. Deaton

King Kong Blues

She couldn't live

This way anymore

A monkey on her back

She said, tired

Hungry and very poor.

The hard rain fell

She said good-bye

I really couldn't tell

If she was truth

Or

I was just a lie.

But,

You know,

I've long had that feeling

I was swinging at planes

From atop

The Empire State Building.

Yeah, So What

What if
What if I were black?
What if
I
Were
Black!
I
I can't
I can't imagine being…
What if I were black…

I would still be me
And fucked.

Steven G. Deaton

Oh, Australia

I have only flirted in passing with this place called Australia.

Was it better to brush lightly against her during one dance or stand still;

waiting for her eyes to meet mine?

The beauty of her supernal gestures lay to rest

all my earthly expectations of this flirtatious adventure;

all too clearly, all too soon.

I should like to climb the rocks again invited,

slowly in time and feel the inland song of wind and tree,

share the water with her as slowly as she shares it

with her lovers. Those creatures that are faithfully hers

can stand there as long as she has

and forever feel the simple truth about her:

What is real and what is not.

That is the gift of her message to you,

patiently inscribed on the walls that are her rocks, rivers and trees.

She is clever enough to keep ready and clear the gift both day and night,

allowing each habit of life the chance to know it over and over again.

Oh, Australia; this is what I found about you.

You were waiting for my eyes to meet yours, not the other way around.

The quiet stillness of your face,

the simple truth to your song,

the definitive nature of your gestures,

play out in perennial chords of color

that can both inspire your lovers and confuse the hurried guest.

I will manage my short affair with her as best I can until

I am quite sure she will lay to rest

her unnatural fear of being misunderstood,

brush off my flirtatious manners,

as she does the hurried traveler,

and give to me another dance.

(1992 Vacation)

Space, A dog on a Leash, A Woman

"Stop Jake!"

"No Jake!"

"Come Here, Jake, Come Here!"

"Okay, Jake, Good Boy!"

Trying to go where no small dog

Had gone before

In the Portland portal

He was a little space shuttle, Columbia,

Running through the cosmic

Or comic

Spheres of doggy curiosity

With a big astronaut tethered in tow.

From one side of the walk

To the other

Sniffing, spraying, and taking mental notes

Least the bombardment of vehicular asteroids

And shooting pedestrians

Sever his lifeline to the towed alien master

And he'll have to command

The trip back to the safety

Of the mother ship alone.

He is a good explorer.

Not afraid of anything

Always ready for a good earthly

Galactic fight.

He jogs with the confidence

That size does not matter

He pees at will

On any monolithic waypoint

He poops in tall grass and open places

He barks and yells at any

Distraction or attraction.

He quenches his thirst at any liquid

Puddle

Or turnout on the journey

Of discovery.

Everything is relative.

He is a giant to the

Creepy sidewalk crawlers

An ant to the planets.

So the risk he takes

Is in the profession he chose:

It's a slow death or a rapid life.

He knows we are no different

Only in kind.

His only obsession: immortality.

He wants to run with

The god of dogs,

Dig in the dirt of hidden bones

Jump at the chance to fetch a stick.

He is just like me,

Only fluffy.

I long to run with god's dog,

Dig in a field of planted flowers

Jump at a chance to fetch a stick:

A token of love

A commitment to infinite possibilities

Of heavenly bonding.

We circle around each other

At a distant gravitational pull

Like Jake running through his space

You being tugged and pulled

Into gentle orbit

And subtle submission.

Separation

The Hale-Bopp

Fly-by

Caused a

Sensational separation

Of God and man

Past the full moon

And total eclipse of the sun.

Those idiots

In San Diego

Chose to

Castrate themselves

In hopes

Of riding the comet

To a starlight Kingdome.

But you and I

Are different

In Portland

Our promise of communion

Is a diamond

To cover all the bases

So, for now

Let's keep everything in tact

You stay with
Your catcher's mitt,
I'll hang onto
My
Balls and bat.

While You're There

Go ahead

Site see.

But don't forget

Whatever evil woman thing

You chose to do

Reflects

Poorly on you

And highly on me.

'Cause I already

Told everybody

You were coming

Naked

And might try

To chastise me.

Oh, yeah,

I warned them.

Flying Home

Over the horizon

The earth

Bends

The light

Into

Blues and reds

And

Hues never realized

In crayon or oils,

Just before the

Dark night

Interrupts

The glory

Of love.

Picasso

Was correct

To celebrate

His beloved whore

On canvas in paint,

For us to enjoy.

One may not

In a lifetime

Completely
Trust the heart,
But at least
He tried.

A Coed After Study Hall

I slipped the car

Into neutral last night

And quietly rolled past your house,

When I thought you'd

Be asleep.

All your lights were out

And your bedroom curtains

Concealed your invitation.

It made me remember

The night you let me in,

Enticing me with your touch.

I watched you sleep

Then drew the curtains closed

Myself certain

Of a second coming.

I know God would

Put a hole in my muffler

If he thought it would help

But last night

I wondered how you slept so well

Cause all things considered,

The hour, the breeze, the dark heat, the stars

The rustling trees

Carried the idle rumble

Whisper from me to you

I slipped the car

Into neutral

And idled past your dreams

I hope the recognizable hum

Of my engine

Woke you anticipatingly up.

(1976)

Outside

Often I can hear

More echoes

Of despair

In your voice

Than I like to feel

Do not humble

Yourself for me

I know where

You've been

You locked your heart

Inside

I am

Outside

Looking in.

(1974)

Untitled

We loved.

We loved so deeply

That it scared the very tissue

Of life

That it grew upon.

Yet we lived.

We lived the very life of love

That lifted our hearts

Together

Through the universe

Tirelessly

Madly twirling about our bodies

Through a timeless love

And unreasoning life.

Love and life;

The life and love

That imitates young passionate lovers,

Those self-forgivers of sin.

While the music of our hearts

And rising souls

Played on,

We danced along the skyway,

The path to the cosmos

Stretched out before us

From the stars to our feet,

And we loved.

(1975)

The Jar of Peanuts

My father says

Peanuts are a mans

Best friend.

The funny thing is

He discovered COSTCO.

Everything big

Everything large.

Everything on sale.

I drove over to

His house

One weekend,

Took Dorothy.

She's my lover

My best friend

My future.

It's the first time

My father met

Someone I could honestly say

I was in love with.

He invited us in

And with paramount enthusiasm

Made coffee

Made conversation

Made years apart

Feel like weeks

Alone.

He was smitten with her

Same as I.

He pointed to his jar

Of COSTCO peanuts

Said we should give the store a try

They have everything

A family needs

In bulk

In selection

In price

The only thing

He was quick to point out

Was the nigger toes in the peanut jar

You had to pick around.

I got an e-mail

From him

A day or two later

He told me everyone

Fell in love with Dorothy

But were concerned about her size,

She's not any bigger then a peanut,

As big as I am

They thought I compromised.

He made sure

He told them all, "She's not tiny,

She's just a little small."

But, "Steve's picked around

In the jar of nuts

Enough to know

A prize from compromise."

He thinks she's

Very pretty

And just the right

Size.

Steven G. Deaton

Athena: Goddess of Reckless Surrender

I surrendered my rights to life and freedom of religious choice last night to the dictatorial command of an Athens taxi driver. I sat without vote at the window seat while he negotiated all Greek triumphs and tragedies with his determined eyes, hands and feet. What skill, what precision, what madness! He alone determined our course through this world. He alone decided if we should both live on the edge of chaotic poetry or let go of our possessions and end everything with one spectacular collision for the innocent bystander. He possessed raw power; simply and deadly. Lights, signs and lines were insubordinate to his authority; testing always. As I watched his world fly by my window I wondered how he chose his companions: Were his calculations based on my and others appearance? Did he rest his head on some woman's shoulder at night? Did he believe in her enough to slip into infinite obscurity with he rest of us? Or did he just become and end in this speeding bullet dodging opportune moped targets until the right one and the right rider presents itself? He would not have made a good soldier in a war. You could give him a dispatch to run to the front, assured it would be received without haste and in the nick-of-time; but you could not count on his return. His recklessness is far more valuable to lose in battle. He would be an intolerable police officer and an uncompromising politician: Too narrow minded, heavy-handed and wrongly opinionated. Both those professions would crucify him. However, his street smart like quick-wit coupled with his surgical skill at running down the intricate nerve endings to the left and the right hemispheres of downtown Athens is evidence enough to support the old saying: Everything and everyone has a place. He, without question, can put a square peg into a round hole! I believe the only flaw in his character, that I could detect, is his unwillingness to call it quits. He used his horn to announce his fast and close intentions instead of his brakes to concede any precious moment of time and occupied space. There was no divine intervention during our journey, no mystics, soothsayers, fortunetellers or good luck charms. No guardian angels or security in seat belts. Only the witness to the pure beauty of speed and slim chances. His dashboard was our altar to it. His windshield our icon. The steering wheel his chalice, his body my Christ, my blood his wine. His right foot on the gas; our confessions. "Fuck Everybody" his gospel. We were praying loud and large through thin cracks in the wind. To the left, to the right, then to the left again. Up, over but never down, and out. We were fucking flying. Flight level: Asphalt. Head strong and at all cost. From the airport to the hotel, he was daring me to lose my lunch as he laughed his way through Athena's purgatory. Cigarette burning in one hand, mobile phone accepting cryptic Grecian commands in the other. He was driving like he was late for his own Olympic funeral and he wanted me to come with him in marathon fashion. The stupid suicidal son-of-a-bitch couldn't do it alone. He was a coward. He needed someone else to add legitimacy to his power and endurance. I had to remind myself to breathe. He gave my life a new predetermined religious purpose: To live again!

"Stop Here!" I cried in prayer.

He paused just long enough at my destination to thank him and to pay a humble sacrifice to his hand. My gift to him was only two thousand drachmas. Not even enough for a decent burial but surely enough for escape from his religion to the safety, security and the freedom in mine. I wanted a receipt. That took time enough for me to stand up taller than his God like position in the drivers seat and made him, for a moment, look up into my eyes so that I could tell him in no uncertain glance that I too could decide his fate. That all six foot four two hundred forty born in the USA pounds of me could slap the crap out of his olive laden dinner size Greek salad feta no cheddar cheese frame if he were to get out of his cab. We shook hands as he handed my proof of passage to me. Kalimera: Have a good day.

I stood at the curb and watched him accelerate, merge and then disappear into the taxi yellow and moped black sea of Athens traffic. I pray he makes it to the front. I think I should frame the receipt. Because, when I look at it, I am reminded of all the precious gifts I have taken for granted in my life and I realize I never want to put you in a position of anything less than total importance to me. I miss America.

An inappropriate laughter at an in excusable time

The Irish whisky

A clock

A calendar doesn't know

'Cause it goes down

young and crispy

old and slow

When the sun

Is high

Or low

In the summer

Or

In the snow.

I would have called you

Sooner

But hell, you really never

Know

What to expect

What to say

What tune to carry

What note to throw away

Loves sleepy music

Plays out hot and cold

Steven G. Deaton

I woke up

Thirsty

Your water glass by my phone

Lipstick smear work comes first

I know

The fire in me

Won't burn

In water

Fuck it's raining outside

Fuck the sun is going to learn

Fuck the day and the hour

I pour myself another mouthful

Of ice and sudden burn.

Depend on the Wind

Did you just feel that?

Easy light wind

From the Northwest?

It gently pushed

My hair to the side

And tried

To lift the back

Of my arms

It swirled about

My legs

But did not

Interfere

With my posture

It guided

Not insulted me.

There's a gypsy laughter

Depending on the wind

Dancing

Enveloping

Sidewalk strollers

Walkers of melancholy

Hearts

Pacers of placid

Minds

Come to think of it

It was you

That forgot to unplug

The coffee pot

Deposit my check

Pick up the dry cleaning

Stop by the liquor store

Get me that thing you said

You were going to

And call in sick for me.

Damn it, Can't you do

Anything right?

Never Praises this Low

Mecca, Medina and Mina

My pilgrimage to Islamic scorn

And Christian contempt

In the desert dilemma of

Husband and wife

Happened all at once

The infidel

On the edge of a cliff

Overlooking

The Muslim pilgrims

Worship

And

Sacrifice

To the beneficent

The almighty

The only one true God

His messenger Mohammad

Made my legs weak

My hands shake

My eyes water

My vision clear

How can I be so wrong?

How can I be so right?

Fear has nothing to do with it

God very little

Salvation everything

First save the soul

The heart will follow

In the night air, dry hot intoxication

My face lifted to the stars

The moon crescent with a strong

Desire

To love, and be free from it.

I fell to my knees

My mind clear

Get the hell out of the Kingdom

Of Saudi Arabia

These people are not like us

They are

Fanatical with self-righteous fatwa

And quick with the sword

My wife, no

My guns

Are padlocked

In a footlocker

In the closet

Of vengeance

Down the hallway of acceptance

Past the door of denial

Across the bedroom of anger

In the house of shock

On the block of adultery

In the neighborhood of

Marriage

In the country of divorce.

I have to do this without

The barrel of lead

Or the blade of steel

But with

The power of the word.

Nothing like it in the world:

Hajj

The gospel and the law,

On their knees

In the desert

Praying

To a woman's earthly

Whisper

And ethereal

Flaw.

Obvious Plans, Hidden Agenda

At the movies

My pager vibrated

Out of respect for the audience.

I had to go

My wife grinned

But her eyes never left the big screen.

The briefing

A lone gunman

Most likely intoxicated, drugged

Found his hunting rife

In his bedroom closet

Pointed it at his mother

Gave her one last chance

To run.

She told the operator

He was a good son

Before the Vietnam War

Before he discovered the liquor stores.

Before his wife left him

Before he lost his one and only job

Before the prescription drugs

Before the restraining order

Before the repossessions

Before the bullets and the gun.

Stop him

But don't hurt him

My orders said

Wake the neighbors up

Before this gets out of hand.

He's my age

He's my life

He's my war

He's the one that didn't survive

The rapid changes

To all our lives.

Fuck him the police said

He won't come out

And he took a shot at one of us.

I pointed a long rifle

At his hidden head

My wife is with her lover

Thinking I'll be all night

They're planning their escape

My mind is racing backwards

I was a good son

Before the Vietnam War

Before I discovered the liquor stores

Before my wife left me for another Joe

Before my car and house

And job became useless

Shelters from the stress and the fire

Storm.

Before the bullets and the gun.

My gun is pointed

In the wrong direction

I see you

I gave him one last chance

To run.

I see you

I see me

"Don't ever hurt me!" My wife cried.

"I won't, I can't, I won't"

I gave her one last chance

To run.

Tribal Commune

Pearl district

Stand on any first Thursday

Corner

Or any day for

That matter

The yeahbutts

The ohyeahs

And the fuegowees

Searching

Fighting

Listing

Painting, buying

And communing

With Portland

And the arts in the pearl.

I saw the ex-governor

Sipping iced tea

She doesn't count

Anymore

What matters now is

Who are you

Where do you live,

In the Gregory?

How much did you pay

Does it include parking

Where do you work

Is it in advertising

Or better yet

Do you own it?

Talk to one of them at

Starbucks, the Paragon

They say

Yeah butt, I'm from Beaverton and

I will some day

Ask one of them at

Terrafazzione, O'ba's

They say

Oh yeah, I have a house in

Lake Oswego

I already made

My fortune

Speak to one of them

In front of Low Brow

Or Late nite dinning at

Touché

They all say

Where the fuck are we?

What matters most

In the Pearl

Is not how you arrived

But how you got here

In second place

And how are you

Goanna stay

In first place.

Silly You, Crazy Me

She wasn't much to look at

I mean

She was Okay

But not grade A

Just a cut above average

In a simple way.

She could walk

Into a room

Unnoticed

Have a conversation

Uninspired

Eat a meal

Not tempted

But she was

In the right place

At the right time

In a silly

Frame of mind.

She had thin red hair

She could do nothing with

Not much

Breast and hip

The waist measured

Almost

Same as the chest.

You could tell

She would have to diet

Her whole life

To keep her ankle size

Down

Her disposition was that

Of a midtown secretary

Over looked

Under appreciated

Under paid

Over worked

Over exaggerated

Her little sister

Still unmarried

Carrying her second child

This one

The father convinced was his

Lucky for her family.

But she had

A gift

Hellishly less than immaculate

And a passion intent on suffocating her

She taught Monica

What a woman's mouth

Was for

I could hardly breathe

While

She fought for air.

We won urgent passion

Extreme freedom

Brave desire

Wanton effect

We lost just cause

I had to have her

Like a dentist

Lives for his niece

Lust describes her cavities

Desire defines his cause

Teeth are pulled

When the Novocain

Takes effect.

She loves me.

She loves me.

She loves what she cannot

She had a silly notion

Only a wild man

Could deceive

The family threat.

I was out

Of my mind

Crazy

When I met her

Should have left

Well enough alone.

But guys are different

Then girls

I could see the good

In her

She thought she could see

The bad

In me.

I was in and out of her life

Like

The air we breathe

Some pure

Some polluted

All necessary

Most evil.

I saw her a few years later

Twin daughters

Lazy husband

She told me he didn't love

Her anymore

But she had her daughters

To care for.

What makes her special

In the land

Of the free and the home

Of the brave

Is being in the right place

At the right time

And knowing what to do

About it

She has her daughters

To love

And care for

She said

There's nothing

NOTHING

Here for

For a crazy man

To live for

Anymore.

The Perennial Clock

It takes two hands

To tell the time

On the

Perennial clock

Of love.

You are

The big hand

Me

The little one

Love

The

Sweep movement.

Now,

Timex sweeps

Jerky

Rolex

Sweeps smooth.

No noticeable change

During the minutes

Hours

Days.

Thank God

For the sunrise

And sunset

Otherwise

My pointer

Your counter

Wouldn't know the sweep difference

Of love

Past the calendar

Of time.

There are no search planes for a survivor like me

It's like I'm stuck in the mud

Of love.

Can't move the vehicle through

To the lighted car wash.

My shoes need polishing and

My pants are dirty.

I got a formal dinner invitation

But I'm miles from nowhere and the road

Is awash and the bridge is out

That's what the radio announcer warned

All travelers on the shortcut road to riches

Just before the battery went dead

I don't have the trunk survival kit

With the flashlight and blanket

My tuxedo is due back

In an hour

There is no way of knowing

If the situation can correct itself

Or if the proper authorities arrived

And fixed the flow of damage unless

I just collect my thoughts

Abandon the vehicle

And start walking out of the mire.

My situation does not warrant brave people

Risking safety and sometimes

Their lives just to find me

Starving

On the wilderness back roads

Of passion postponed.

I must walk out of the forest

Of confusion

On my own merit.

You are already there, home,

Waiting at the table

You give me strength to endure

I may not make it to dinner tonight

But the thought of your nourishing food

Makes my milky way

Turn to energy bar.

I've been without transportation

Before,

It can be done.

There are so many other

Attractive alternatives available

To the weary traveler

That the purchase of a particular make

Or model

Seems an idea borne of the ad age

Not of the

Information age.

Information is to power

As is power to seduction

Both can be infinitely helpful and dreadfully sorrowful

To the point of wishing

They had never met.

Especially in one infinitesimal mostly insignificant life.

The small people

Don't understand power

Sometimes the big people don't either

It crushes the small

And distills the big

They recover with manufactured respect

And sheltered incentives.

But the small salvage

Self-esteem and pride, and a purpose.

I am small but my love

Big, my information correct.

My power an illusion for so long

And a dreadful mire forever.

I will walk home.

It will be a long walk home,

But one with dignity:

Wandering and wondering.

Nothing Keeps Happening

Politics are being played

Even while you read

This.

It's not enough

Anymore

To be satisfied

Wanting more.

I've been through

A hell of a lot

Of this and of that

I keep coming back

To the fact

That this life

Isn't worth

Compromise   Synthesize   Fraterize   Emphasize

Situationalize   Harmmonize   Fractionalize   Criticize

Departmentalize   Developmentalize   Computerize

Legalize   Institutionalize   Minimize   Industrialize

Miniaturize   Informationalize   Customize

Constitutionalize   Finalize   Dogmatize   Materialize

Burglarize   Strategize   Patronize   Economize

Compartmentalize   Itemize   Capitalize   Energize

Televise   Notarize   Soliloquize   Environmentalize
Polarize   Naturalize   Ostracize   Maximize   Reutilize
Idealize   Winterize   Personalize   Sensationalize
Prioritize   Epitomize   Scrutinize   Characterize   Idolize
Penalize   Alphabetize   Circumcise   Memorize   Satirize
Immunize   Spiritualize   Colorize   Antagonize   Polarize
Pulverize   Acclimatize   Rationalize   Pasteurize
Exercise   Familiarize   Hypnotize   Americanize
Specialize   Sodomize   Centralize   Equalize   Optimize
Deodorize   Attitudinize   Rubberize   Neutralize
Globalize   Formalize   Proselytize   Caramelize
Conceptualize   Terrorize   Apologize   Criminalize
Mesmerize   Standardize   Generalize   Mobilize
Sympathize   Civilize   Scrutinize   Socialize   Vitalize
Totalize   Cannibalize   Localize   Bastardize   Theorize
Containerize   Hypnotize   Dramatize   Agonize
Plagiarize   Antagonize   Gelatinize   Brutalize
Monopolize   Notarize   Prophesize   Verbalize
Legitimize   Visualize   Vocalize   Anesthetize
Hospitalize   Symbolize   Supersize   Sanitize
Materialize   Victimize
Womanize
Demilitarize
Memorialize
Individualize
Recognize the

Compromise

Before you aggrandize

The son's bitches

That

Politicize and

Philosophizes

Nothing

Keeps happening

The more you

Realize is.

It's that January Simple

I'd like to describe the perfect woman

And see if you agree.

Singing

Outside my winter window

There is a yellow breasted

Western Meadowlark

Nesting

On a barren old oak tree

Holding

The bird on high

With a promise of spring.

When all she really had

To do

Was just say

Yes to me.

Steven G. Deaton

Nobody, wrong number

The afternoon sun shines

Straight through your high hopes

And lights the shaded

Bedroom of passion.

How is that empty room

To sleep in?

Portland isn't working

For us.

One of us has to move

Further North

Seattle, that's where

All the misfits are

Before they have to go on to

Alaska.

We can blend.

Going, going

Gone man the first sign:

Giving shit away.

Crazy people give everything away,

Even each other.

The second sign:

The long distance phone calls

To people in your address book

With about three or four

Crossed out addresses

Covering several states.

Track'em down

It's extremely important

At three thirty in the morning

Just before the last half-a-shot

Of wine is in the glass

And you're trying to make

The cigarette and the drink

End even

The operators voice sounds

Better then the wife

I can't remember

Even if it's electronic bullshit voice

Simulated

Why don't you answer me

Do you love me

Yes or no?

Fuck it, I'll hang up on the information age

Trip the bleep beep bitch up

She can give the number

Of ol'what's her face

To the dial tone.

The third sign:

More pronounced then

The first and the second

The man is always trying

To get naked.

Can't seem to be confined

In garmets

Always shedding layers.

You've got to stay on your toes

Clothes can come off quick.

In a restaurant

It's harder then hell

To get the crazy person

Dressed again

Especially if you embarrass easily

The waiter's laugh

As they dial 911

The atomic operator says give me Steve

They say

Hey man, this calls for you

It's the satellite bitch

Still trying to get me that number

I requested

Just before the cigarette and the wine

Ended even Steven

And I said fuck it

Went to bed naked

She found me

And will never let it rest

Because she is electric

You can't stop electrons positively charged

Even if you knew how

She says for an extra fifty cents

She can connect the call

For me

I don't even have to write the number down

Or dial

I say

Are you naked

She says press one for yes

Two for no

I press one and hang up

again

Because I don't even know

Who I was trying to call or why

After all these years she might not

Remember

Or act like she doesn't

If her husband says from his bed of

Shaded passion

Who the hell is calling at this hour?
Oh, nobody, wrong number.

Steven G. Deaton

RawHeyHoe

I get a dispatch

To the house

Where

A black man is pissed

And

Confused.

Park the police cruiser

Next to the

Curb

A few houses away

Walk

Low and slow

To the address

Over the radio.

Nothing

Out of place

Nothing

To be afraid of

I unsnap my

Holster

Knock on the door.

A little kid answers

Doesn't say anything

Nods

Come on in.

I watch him

Go back to his three friends

Sit'n in front of the TV

Bugs bunny

Beat'n Elmer Fudd

The cop

To the carrot and the

Hole.

I stand in the doorway

Look past the table

To my left into the

kitchen

And see this caricature of

A black grandma

Stirring the pot

Nothing to be afraid of.

Coming down the hall

Agitated

Angry

Yelling at me

A black man

Me without the badge

Screaming

Something about

The bitch.

No one flinches

Except me.

My holster is unsnapped

Already

I am a white man

In the black man's shit

But I have a way out

Of it

Save the witnesses

And the kids

And the grandma cookin

Something good.

He says:

Arrest her

Sheebee rawheyhoe.

I say what?

He says

Sheebee rawheyhoe.

I say calm down

Relax

Take a deep breath

He says fuck that.

Bugs and Elmer

Are still at it

The rabbit

Manages to thump the fudd cop.

The grandma keeps stirring the pot.

I take out my notebook

Say again

So I can write a report

Sheebee rawhayhoe.

I can't write what he says

I am a fudd in the wabbit hole

And grandma ain't cook'n grits for me.

None of those kids

Can help me

Except to keep the angry man

At home.

I say sir

I don't understand

You will have to talk slower

Calmer

And easy

Include me

Don't……

Before I can finish

The kid that answered the door

Turned around from the TV

To look at me

Grandma

Stepped out of

Her past

To counsel me

She said

Politely, succinctly

"Officer, my son's woman; she's

a rock head whore. You do understand,

Don't you?"

Fudd and the wabbit

Same carrot, same hole.

"Yes ma'am. I do."

That was the only

Time

In my life

The words

"I do"

made perfect

Sense.

I know what I'm trying to say

Don't confuse me.

I won't understand

Or stand

For it.

I do not

Adapt to change

Very well

Or not

At all.

I have a routine

Of beliefs

And of

Work and play.

What ever it is

You are trying to tell

Me

Or

Convince me of

Is not going

To happen.

It doesn't take an

Ad man

Or

Regis

Who wants to be him

Anyway

To tell me

About money

About life

About love

About me

About home

About shirts and ties

I am about ME

And Had it

With your whole programming

Poles

With an error margin

Big enough to drive

All the car commercials

Through

And the experts

With teeth shinny

Enough

To attract trout to

I've been fly fish'n

Wade out

Not to deep

Cast across shallow water

Tease

A little bit

Snag snooker

Reel'm in.

Thump'm

Measure'm

Tag'm

Polaroid'm

Throw'm

Back in.

Retire for the weekend

Grin'n

Drink'n

Hand shake'n

Get back to the office

And start

Again.

Okay,

It's Okay.

Leave me alone,

I know what I'm doing

I know what

I'm trying

To say

I don't need another car

And the girls

Don't really look

Like that.

And if they do

Trump, Sheen, Costner,

Clooney, Pitt, Clinton, and Condit

Already

did it.

Sleep'n Mean Jesus

(Vietnam, 1971-1972)

Ain't no foolin

Da buther's

Thaze wake'n up

Dead

Ain't nuttin

U-se could be do'n bout it.

Cept'n

Praise it wasn't U.

Jus fuc-kin

Which ya

Dat's it

Da Deb-el

Jus fuc-kin

Which ya.

Hey man, U-got a-nudder

Kool

Pass it here.

Dis white man's

Muth-er fuc-kin

Army

Ain't no

Plaze for a

Beautiful

Black man.

Yeah, I mean me

Dis ain't

No muth-er fuc-kin plaze

Foe me

Da white man's

Deb-el

He be dressed like

Da muth-er fuc-kin ker-nel

Been shout'n

Mount up

Lock'n load

Like dat fuc-kin

Charlie muth-er fuc-ker

Be scared

Not me, no sir, not me

Dis ain't no

Muth-er fuc-kin plaze

Foe a

Beautiful

Black man like me.

Pass

Dat muth-er fuc-kin

Kool

Ov'r here

Or U

Gonna be

Wak'n up

Dead.

Muth-er fuc-ker

Drag

Dat fuc-kin Kool

Down

Two da

Deb-el's own

Siagon

Muth-er fuck-in slant eyed

Pussy be side-waze

Dat's rite

Ain't no shit

Side-waze muth-er fuck-er

Here

It's a fuck-in cigarette

U kracker muther-fuc-kin

Ass-hole

Dat ker-nel

Prob-la-be U-r daddy

Cept'n

I know he be U-r mamma

And I got

Steven G. Deaton

His
Mount up'n
Rite here.
Drag on it
u-cum-bat muth-er fuc-ker
Sleep'n mean Jesus
U-gonna
Wake up
Dead
Any waze.

Shanghaied penis

It's me

Steve,

Take your clothes off.

This is damn near rape,

Date,

Turned to favor

Tricked to labor

We just met

Can you do that?

Yes, I can.

It was that

Easy

And wait till

You see

What's under the

Zipper

Throbbing, harder than

The time it took

To get your

Address

More determined

To undermine

Your vows

Then Victoria's

Secret

Wish

To conquer

My main little

Man.

It started as

Adolescent experimentation

Evolved to

College free for all

Bachelor's degree

Developed into

Marriage obligation

And

Monogamist hypnotism

Turned into

Divorce

Decree

Sherman's march to the

Sea

Burn down every house

From

Age 18 thru 33.

Was a trick

A ploy

A game to play

And well rehearsed.

I had a secret wish

Once

But it came true

And now

It's work; and

A blessed

Curse.

Steven G. Deaton

F O M B

Every woman

Nowadays

Have 1.2 kids.

Daughters mostly.

NO

Husband

Some have

A woman friend

That calls regularly

Somewhat athletic looking

If not by

Oddball sports

Then certainly

A couple of bar fights

For the record, physically constructed

For one purpose,

Genetically engineered for another

Trying to reinvent

Normal

Acceptable

Mutually beneficial

Relationships

For the

1.2 kids.

I've stayed away

From the woman with kids

As long as I could

But now

That's all there is.

The mating ritual

For older greyhounds and

Slower foxes

Who still believe

In opposite sex romances

Requires more skill,

Dialog and tolerance

From the man in the den

More often then not

She wants a complete

Notarized

Copy of the pedigree

Describing me.

Point to a picture

Of another man

The subject changes

To the other women

Around town

Like her

That say,

Oh, I'm not in love with him

He ain't even my ex-

He's just a friend

And I'm always nice to him

'Cause maybe,

Could be maybe,

He's

The father of my baby.

The Enigmatic Nature of the Invisible Finish Line

Hurry up and wait

Every soldier knows the drill

Generals

Probably invented it

To keep the restless

Privates still

Fallacious magnates

Borrowed it

To make the hungry consumers

Pay

All in order to instill

A sense of purpose and resolve

In the human race

To acquire and accumulate,

To sleep, eat, reproduce, work and to play.

Life is a portrait

Of luck, love, (blank), chance and risk

The puzzle piece

Left out of the box

Just spiritually happens to be

Invisible

Can't you see?

No one knows, I mean

No one knows

What the big picture means

Or what thousand words it's trying to say.

Save for a select few

Exceptions, we elect

Unfair

Not right

Lucky bastards

Why not me

How come?

Look at the food pyramid, not the sacraments,

Not for the answer

But for a clue:

The opinion of the onion

Cries the tomato

Is that the difference

Between

Apples and oranges, is currency not,

But the wholesome

apricot.

It satisfies the halves;

For the have nots,

It's the pits.

Think on it,

Think hard.

Episodes

Our love

Has not been satisfied

By any definition

The explanation of it

Can only be reasoned

From the light and the dark

Episodes

Down in the

River canyons

Screaming shadows

Echoes

Of

Single-minded compromise

High desert plateaus

Presenting

Mumbling silhouettes

Of honest remorse

And ceaseless wonder.

Only the desire

Has been tempered

By a more livable cool concern

For the consequences

Of the fever passion

Branded on our souls

Like a prisoner boxed

In four stone walls

Stick scratching

Another diagonal line

Across the previous four days

I am either counting

Strength up

Each day

Sentenced served

Screaming

In the canyon

Of liquid darkness, tortuous happiness

And amorous anger

Or I am counting down

Each day stronger

Lighter

In quiet remembrances

Towards definition

Steven G. Deaton

It tragically ends where it usually euphorically begins

And vice versa

Is the situation reserved

For relationships.

She said that

No I did

She did that

No I did

I wanted this and that

No she did

I thought…

No, I didn't think

She thought…

No, she misunderstood.

I bought it for you

I didn't know

You already had one

Or two

It meant everything to me

And nothing to you

How would I know

Same way you do

Guess, probe, ponder, hope and assume

Maybe this will be

Different

In the same expectatious way

Of all the others

I showed you mine

You showed me yours

Somehow

Everything else doesn't matter

Until

Everything else seems to matter

Same way it did

Before

Me

Before

You

Before

Eve said yes to the

Bite of the apple

And

Adam

Said yes

To the

Taste of the

Forbidden fruit.

All I ever

Wanted

Was all I

Ever

Wanted

And

Vice versa.

About the Author

Steven G. Deaton was born in California on Veterans Day, 1950. He received his Bachelors Degree in Political Science from California State University, Chico, 1981. His professional career has spanned from police work where he served as an Officer with the City of Ashland, Oregon, Police Department and was a member of the Special Emergency Reaction Team with the Portland Police Bureau to 22 years as a United States Army Aviator. While with the U.S. Army, and the Oregon Army National Guard, Steve has flown combat missions as an aircraft commander in the Republic of Vietnam, served in the Korean Cold War as a combat surveillance pilot, and voluntarily served as an aircraft commander flying a utility cargo airplane in Operation Desert Storm.

Currently, Steve serves as a Captain for an east coast based airline, and lives in Portland, Oregon.